WILD AND WEIRD PETS

Helen Chapman

CONTENTS

Introduction	4
Spiders	6
Stick Insects	14
Geckos	22
Glossary/Index	32

WILD AND WEIRD PETS

Is your idea of a pet something cute and cuddly – something you can stroke, that will come when you call? If so, these weird and wonderful pets are not for you. These pets are more likely to be slinky, or stick-like, and have a diet of mice and insects! And they all shed their skins.

In this book you will find information on 3 interesting pets – a tarantula, a stick insect and a gecko. You'll learn about their **natural habitats** and how to own and care for them. By the end you'll have looked at the good things and the bad things about keeping **exotic** pets.

SPIDERS

ABOUT SPIDERS

Trappers and Hunters

There are two main spider types. One type traps its food in a web, while the other type hunts it. The hunters stalk their prey, pounce on them and bite them with poison fangs.

This spider stalks and jumps.

This spider traps its prey in a web.

In the United Kingdom there are about 36 trillion – that's 36 million billions – individual spiders. This means there are 600,000 spiders for every person in the country!

What Spiders Do

Never kill a spider, just because you can. The planet needs spiders. They have all kinds of uses.

- The big hunter spiders eat pests like locusts and mice that harm crops.
- Smaller spiders keep the place clean by eating insects like flies that carry diseases.
- Spiders are food for birds, lizards, small mammals, wasps and others.
- Spiders help **fertilize** plants by carrying pollen and seeds on their bodies.

Spider silk is wonderful stuff. It is stronger than steel and more stretchy than elastic. We are learning how it works so we can copy it.

A spider eating a locust

LOOKING AFTER A TARANTULA

Why Keep a Tarantula?

Tarantulas are the spiders most likely to be kept as pets. They are quiet and don't need very much space. What do they do? Not a lot during the day! They are **nocturnal**. You must watch them at night.

Spider and babies by their burrow

What Does a Tarantula Need?

Your spider needs to be comfortable. Learn about its natural home, and copy this as best you can. Some tarantulas live off the ground, and some live on the ground or in holes. Some live in forests and some live in deserts. But all tarantulas are good climbers and like to move around.

This spider lives in the desert.

This spider lives in a forest.

WHAT TARANTULAS NEED

Make Your Tarantula a Home

A tarantula can live in almost any container. Make sure its home has a strong top, so that it cannot escape. It will need airholes to let in oxygen and help keep the air damp.

- A **vivarium** gives it room to move about.

- Put in a branch it can climb along.

- Put some sandy soil or peat in the bottom.

- Give it somewhere to hide! Half a flowerpot or a piece of bark is perfect.

- Tarantulas need water, so provide a plastic lid as a water dish. Put some pebbles in to stop it tipping over.

Feeding your Tarantula

In the wild, tarantulas hunt and kill. They eat mice, insects, moths and small reptiles. As pets, tarantulas need to be fed live food. You can buy 'pinkies' – three-day-old mice – crickets and worms at most pet and bait shops. Tarantulas also eat other tarantulas – so don't put two together!

1. Feed your tarantula once a week.

2. Remove any food that the tarantula doesn't eat after a day or two.

3. Keep the water dish filled up with clean water.

4. Mist its home with water twice a week.

A well-stocked tarantula home

WHAT ARE THE RISKS?

To you:
All tarantulas bite and all carry **venom**. Some shoot hairs from their **abdomen** when they are afraid. These can pierce your skin and burn you.

To your tarantula:
Female tarantulas in the wild can live for up to 20 years. So don't take one on if you aren't ready to have it as part of your life for a long time.

Put your hand in front of it.

Oh, no! What's happening to Fluffy?

Week 1. Something's wrong. Fluffy's not eating her crickets!

Week 2. Fluffy's making a web. Now she's lying on her back.

Week 3. I've worked out what's wrong. She's starting to moult.

Week 4. This'll take ages. I can't touch her. She might get stressed and die.

Dos and don'ts

Don't: Pick up a tarantula.
Do: Put your hand in front of where it wants to go. This way it thinks that being on your hand is its idea – and it probably won't bite!

Don't: Touch a tarantula when it lifts its front legs. It is scared and may attack.
Do: Watch your spider's body language. It will show you how it feels.

Don't: Let your tarantula fall. Its abdomen could burst and it could die.
Do: Keep it away from high places like your lap.

Body language says "Back off!"

Week 5. Fluffy's nearly shed her old skin. Soon she'll be as good as new.

She's moulting!

STICK INSECTS

STICK INSECTS IN THE WILD

Look! Up in the tree. Is it a branch? Is it a twig? No, it's a stick insect! All 3,000 species of stick insects look like sticks! No surprise there. But what is surprising is that they are one of the most popular insects to be kept as pets. Is it because they cost nothing to feed? Is it because they don't make a mess, or smell? Probably. But it's more likely to be because they have very special talents.

Special Talent No.1

Stick insects are masters of disguise. It's hard to spot a stick insect unless you look closely. In a garden or a jungle, their body shape and brown or green colour help them to hide. When still, stick insects put their front legs in front of their head. They become like part of the plant, twig or branch. When they move, the insects sway to look like a stick being blown by the wind.

Special Talent No.2

Stick insects are only active at night. If you live in the right part of the world – Australia or New Zealand, for example – you can grab a torch, go outside and take a look. You may see one! They feed at night when **predators** like birds are asleep. And they always eat their greens! A half eaten leaf with bite marks shows a predator where they are, so the stick insects eat all the leaf.

HOW STICK INSECTS STAY ALIVE

Stick insects are found in bushes and trees. They are fragile, so they have some strange ways of escaping danger. They are good at avoiding being seen by other animals that hunt them. This means that they can survive in lots of different and difficult situations.

When chased, a stick insect can lose a leg. The predator stops and eats the leg instead of the insect. Young stick insects can even grow another leg!

Who'd want to eat a stick insect? This spider would!

This stick insect flashes the dark spots on its back legs and the bright red colour under its wings — a warning sign.

This one flaps its wings and spins quickly on the ground to scare its attacker.

It sprays its droppings far away from its home to fool the hunter.

STICK INSECTS AS PETS

It's best to buy stick insects from a good breeder. If you live in a country where they live in the wild, never take them from their natural environment. If you live in a country where stick insects are exotic imports, never set them free. Either way, you could upset a fragile **ecosystem**.

Don't: Crowd the cage. The insects will fight. They may even eat each other if they don't have enough space, water or food.
Do: Put them with only a couple of other stick insects.

Don't: House them in a low cage. They need room to hang, moult and grow.
Do: Make sure the height of the cage is at least three times the length of an adult stick.

Don't: Get the insects wet. They breathe through their bodies and could drown.
Do: Spray just the cage and the leaves once a day.

Use a tall jar.

Mist daily.

Don't: Put the cage in sunlight.
Do: Sit the cage under a light bulb to keep the insects warm. A red light is best, as the light won't disturb the stick insects at night, but make sure they can't touch it, or they may burn themselves.

Warm with a red bulb.

Don't: Feed the insects leaves that may have been sprayed with chemicals.
Do: Feed them fresh blackberry, bramble or privet leaves. Keep the leaves on the branches and stand them in a jar of water.

Feed with fresh leaves.

A well-equipped home

WHY KEEP STICK INSECTS

Although keeping stick insects takes care and effort, it can be very rewarding. Stick insects won't love you in the way that dogs and cats do, but they are interesting to watch. Here is what one person said: "I have found walking sticks to be fascinating insects. They are colourful, easy to keep, and useful for teaching both students and the general public about insects, science and nature."

What are the Risks?

To you:
- Some stick insects can hurt you! The Thorn Legged Stick will pinch and bite. The American Walking Stick sprays a chemical that can cause short-term blindness and pain.

To the stick insect:
- Stick insects are delicate and easily lose legs. It is best not to touch them.

- The RSPCA says not to breed stick insects (although if you are looking after them properly, it is likely that they will lay lots of eggs). It is very hard to find good homes for young ones.

Fascinating to watch

THE STICK INSECT LIFE CYCLE

Stick insects grow by moulting. They shed their skins about five times, and come back bigger each time. They need a twig to hang from, so they can crawl down out of the old skin. After the fifth moult (called an "instar") they are adult. The males have wings, the females can start to lay eggs.

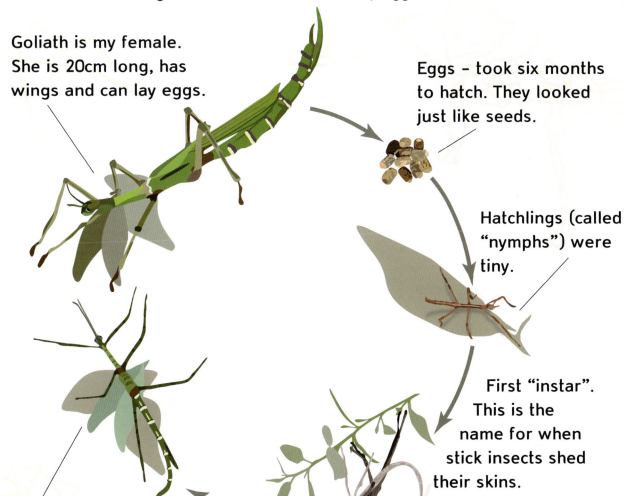

Goliath is my female. She is 20cm long, has wings and can lay eggs.

Eggs – took six months to hatch. They looked just like seeds.

Hatchlings (called "nymphs") were tiny.

First "instar". This is the name for when stick insects shed their skins. It happens five times.

David is my adult male. A male is half the size of a female, but has longer feelers.

Geckos

Geckos as pets

Geckos are lizards, but they are lizards in a class of their own. What makes them so amazing? Unlike other lizards, geckos have vocal cords. They chirp like birds, some even bark. They also shed their skins once a month, which is fascinating to watch. Geckos like to stay in the one place. They also like to be alone. They are just as happy in a cage as in the wild – as long as they are looked after properly.

Geckos galore

The gecko family includes more than 700 species – 20% of all the world's lizards! Their size ranges from 3 cm to 35 cm. They have eyes as sharp as a cat's, and can see better than any other lizard.

Yellow-bellied house geckos

Get a grip!

Some geckos have a cool trick. They can run upside down along a ceiling or straight up a window. They have special tiny, brush-like claws under their toes that help them to grip smooth surfaces. Their grip is so strong, that even a fat gecko can support its own weight with just one toe!

Knob-tailed gecko

Geckos in their natural habitat

Geckos are found in rocky deserts and semi-arid grassland all over the world. They escape the heat of the day by hiding in cracks and burrows. At night they come out to hunt for food. Their skin colour matches the area where they live. This helps them surprise prey and hide from **predators** like snakes and birds. Geckos are important to the environment as they help control the insect population.

New Zealand gecko in flowers

Leopard gecko in the wild

LEOPARD GECKOS

Leopard geckos are the perfect reptile pets. They have a gentle nature and rarely bite. They become very tame and may take food from your fingers and sit on your shoulder, but they do need careful looking after.
Leopard geckos have dark brown spots on white or pale yellow. They are usually 15 to 22 cm long.

Leopard geckos are found in Pakistan, India and Afghanistan.

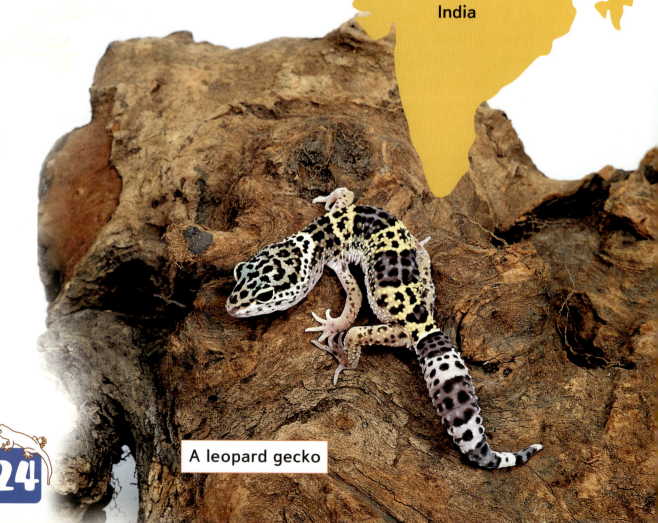

A leopard gecko

A secret weapon

A gecko's tail is very cleverly designed. It has lots of different uses. For instance, leopard geckos store fat in their tails, and live on this when food is scarce. Like other lizards, the gecko has a tail that will break off in an enemy's claws. The gecko runs free just when the enemy pounces, leaving its tail behind. Later on, the tail grows back, although it never looks quite as good again, and the gecko goes hungry for a while without its foodstore. This is how it works:

Losing a tail

The tail breaks at a crack in the backbone.

The surrounding muscles are arranged to separate.

A muscle closes around the artery at the point of the break. This stops blood loss.

The gecko grows a new tail.

CARING FOR YOUR GECKO

You will need

Make your gecko's home as like its natural home as you can. Put in rocks, branches, sand and leaves to give shelter.

Never keep more than one male in a tank: they will fight, sometimes to the death.

Keep your tank warm with a heat pad. Put a red bulb above the tank at one end. Your gecko will enjoy the warmth, and you will enjoy watching it at night.

Put a hiding place at each end, one dry and one full of damp material for the gecko to hide in. Spray the damp one with water every day. This will help your gecko to keep its skin moist so it can shed it easily.

It will also need a shallow water dish, like a plastic lid, weighted down with a stone.

You can buy live crickets to feed your gecko. Some people dust these with vitamin supplements to keep their geckos healthy.

A well-stocked vivarium

What are the Risks?

Risks to you:

Geckos may carry a disease called salmonella. You can catch it by not washing your hands properly when you have been touching your gecko or its tank.

Risks to your gecko:

Geckos in the wild can live from 10 to 20 years, so don't take them on if you aren't prepared to make them part of your life for a long time.

Geckos are delicate little creatures. For instance, you may need to gently help them to shed their skin. If it's too dry, it won't come off properly, but you mustn't pull it or the new skin underneath will tear.

A Northland Green gecko sheds its skin.

MY LEOPARD GECKO SPOT

This is an 11-month-old leopard gecko called Spot. He is about 23 cm long, and his owner can understand his body language. His owner says:

" When Spot wants out of his cage, he scratches on the side, or climbs up high.

When I walk in the room, he looks at me, and when I stick my hand into his cage, he licks my hand and walks onto it. He only does that with me.

Spot loves being lightly misted with a squirt bottle. He licks the water off his nose. It is very cute.

When I talk to him, he opens his eyes wide and looks at me. He recognizes his name, my voice, and me!

When Spot gets tired he half closes his eyes. When he's alert or hunting his eyes get big. I can always tell what type of mood he's in. "

KEEPING EXOTIC PETS

Arguments rage about the **ethics** of keeping exotic pets. If you look on the Internet you will find websites set up by people who have really enjoyed observing and caring for pets like leopard geckos, and who want to share their enthusiasm with others. These may turn out to be the naturalists of the future.

FOR

- People who keep exotic pets develop skills of patient observation which help them to understand how animals function.

- Some creatures are so threatened in the wild that keeping them as pets is the only way to guarantee their safety.

- If local people are making a living from collecting wild creatures, they will look after the forests, instead of clearing them to plant crops.

- It is better to experience looking after an animal yourself than watching it in the wild on TV.

Better than watching TV!

At the same time, organizations such as the RSPCA and Animal Aid have expressed doubts about the wisdom of keeping exotic creatures as pets. Too often they die of stress very quickly. Here are some of the arguments. What do you think?

AGAINST

- Many rare creatures have a miserable life before dying in the hands of people who don't know how to look after them.

- The main threat to exotic species in the wild is being captured and sold for money to people who want to keep them as pets.

- The trade in wild creatures brings smugglers billions of dollars a year, and is not properly regulated.

- It's cruel to keep wild animals imprisoned for our pleasure.

Is this what we were born for?

GLOSSARY

abdomen the bigger of a spider's two body parts

ecosystem natural balance, in which every plant and creature has enough space

ethics the right way to behave

exotic foreign and exciting

fertilize help plants grow

fragile easily broken

locust large grasshopper

natural habitat wild home

nocturnal active at night

predators creatures that kill to eat

venom poison

vivarium tank for your creature to live in

vocal cords they help you to speak

INDEX

geckos 22–23, 28
habitats
   geckos 23
   stick insects 14
   tarantulas 9
leopard geckos 24–29
   defence 25
   keeping 26–27
   risks 28
lizards 22
moulting
   geckos 28
   stick insects 21
   tarantulas 12–13
spider silk 7
spiders 6
   in UK 6
Spot (leopard gecko) 29
stick insects 14–21
   defence 14–17
   keeping 18–19
   life cycle 21
   risks 20
tarantulas 8–9
   keeping 10–11
   risks 12–13